PRAGUE
CASTLE

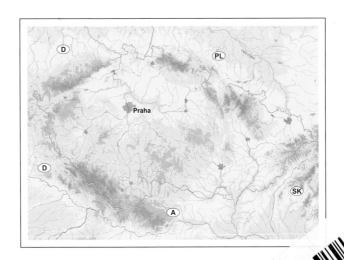

uniosguide

INTRODUCTION

The Prague Castle complex is a paramount historical monument of the Czech Republic and also has been a symbol of Czech nationality for centuries. St. Vitus' Cathedral, where a sacred place for Czechs, the Chapel of St. Wenceslas, is located dominates the complex. The Czech royal crown jewels have been enshrined in a chamber over the chapel. The castle complex, representational seat and the largest in the entire country, is surrounded with charming palaces and magnificent royal gardens, which underlines its special charm. All architectural styles have left their imprint on Prague Castle, beginning with the Romanesque era. Outstanding European artists contributed to today's appearance of the complex and have created a work of art that ranks among the most important items of world cultural heritage. In 1992, the Prague Castle complex was placed on the UNESCO World Heritage List together with the historical Prague centre. This publication aims to acquaint you with the history of Prague Castle and to provide you with a brief outline of its sights. We wish you many pleasant experiences.

The editors

PRAGUE CASTLE

Publisher: Unios CB spol. s r. o.
MCU vydavatelství Unios, Hany Kvapilové 10, 370 10 České Budějovice,
Tel./fax: +420 387 428 360, e-mail: vydavatelstvi@unios.cz, www.unios.cz
Technical editors: Pavel Dvořák, Radek Eliášek, Petr Steinbauer
Text: Viktor Kubík
Translation: Překladatelský servis skřivánek s. r. o. – Blanka Petáková, Steve Johnstone
Photographs: Libor Sváček, Miroslav Hucek, Jiří Podrazil, Photo archives of Prague Castle
Pre-press layout of the photographs: Libor Sváček, Jiří Kořan
Maps: SHOCart Zlín
Commercial presentation: MCU vydavatelství Unios, Marek Otípka, Magdalena Votavová
Typesetting and printing: Typodesign, s. r. o., České Budějovice, Jiří Kořan
Distribution: GeoClub, s. r. o.; www.geoclub.cz
Prague – tel.: +420 283 890 152, fax: +420 283 890 153, e-mail: praha@geoclub.cz
Brno – tel.: +420 545 229 343, fax: +420 545 229 345, e-mail: brno@geoclub.cz
MCU velkoobchod Unios; tel., fax: +420 387 428 360, e-mail: velkoobchod@unios.cz
MCU Praha, s. r. o.; tel.: +420 283 893 146, e-mail: mcu.praha@unios.cz

1ˢᵗ edition, České Budějovice 2003
10ᵗʰ publication in the Uniosguide series, 64 pages

ISBN 80-7339-017-5
ISBN 80-7339-016-7 (angl. vyd.)

Prague Castle complex – bird's-eye view

PRAGUE CASTLE

Prague and Prague Castle are two inseparable terms. The history of the city and the castle are closely connected and make up a complex mixture of historical, political, and social events. The question may arise as to which existed first: the city or the castle? In trying to answer this question we will encounter the well-known dilemma of the chicken and the egg, but the fact is that the life and history of the city and the castle are interwoven, have influenced each other for centuries, and cannot be separated.

The elevated site that stands over the Vltava River has attracted the attention of settlers since time immemorial. The place is naturally bordered and protected from all sides, which makes it a strategic point: the Brusnice Brook borders the rocky elevation to the north (today the brook runs through Stag Moat {Jelení příkop}), the hill slopes down steeply to the Vltava to the south and east, and a gap separated the site from the Hradčany area to the west. Two springs supplied the settlers with water on the rocky plateau – the well of St. Wenceslas and a subterranean spring, today flows under the central castle wing (in front of the Golden Gate of St. Vitus´ Cathedral). Both springs were used as wells. Rich arenaceous marl and sandstone mines were situated to the

Prague's historical centre – view from St. Vitus' Cathedral

Night view of Prague Castle and the Charles Bridge

southwest and west, and the castle was protected against cold winds by the rocky massif of Petřín to the south.

Traces of the oldest settlement were mostly destroyed by later building activities and the oldest history is documented by archaeological finds not directly from the site itself, but in the surrounding areas and near the historical town center.

Prague is situated in roughly the center of Bohemia at the intersection of ancient trade routes. This crossroads attracted new settlers as early as primeval times, which is documented by a Paleolithic settlement in Přezletice, Nebušice and Řevnice (from 700 000 – 20 000 BC) and by Neolithic treasures from Dejvice and Stromovka (dating back to the 5th millennium BC). The ancient cultures of Řivnáče and Únětice created important centers that influenced the development of the whole country. Traces of the first settlement on the Prague Castle plateau date back to the 3rd millennium BC. From that time on, the area and the neighboring Hradčany district have been continually settled.

Závist hill over Zbraslav on the southern outskirts of Prague became an important site for the Celts. A large settlement (later an opidum) was built here in the 5th century BC and remained in existence until the first century AD. This place was of enormous importance not only for our country, but for the whole of Central Europe (which is documented, for example, by the tomb of a rich noblemen that was excavated in Bubeneč). The complex covered 170 hectares and comprised a sanctuary and nine-kilometer-long fortifications (the most ingenious in

Changing of the guard

Northern entrance to Prague Castle over the Powder Bridge

St. Wenceslas' helmet

the ancient Celtic world), which indicates the future importance of Prague and Prague Castle. Závist probably became the seat of the famous Langobard king Wach. The Celts were replaced by the ancient Slavs, who moved their settlements closer towards today's Prague center and Prague Castle. The 6th century saw flourishing development in Roztoky u Prahy and in Šárka. In the 8th century and beyond, many towns and villages (e.g. Budeč, Levý Hradec, Tetín) were founded and a market place sprang up in the region of today's Lesser Town (Malá Strana), together with a settlement in the Hradčany region. And so the area of the future Prague Castle gained its political importance and cult status.

Old Royal Palace - Romanesque floor

Archeological research and the oldest written sources indicate that Prague Castle was probably founded in the year 880 by Prince **Bořivoj** of the Přemyslid dynasty. Bořivoj built a castle, founded the Church of the Virgin Mary (the second oldest church in Bohemia) and moved his seat from Levý Hradec to Prague. Archaeological finds have also proven that the Prague Castle elevation became the Bohemian iconic and political center before 850 AD, which partly corresponds to legends told by the ancient chronicler Christian (the end of the 10th century). The place served as a meeting point for the Czech nobility, who here elected their Prince and enthroned him. At the same time, the Žiži hillock served as an iconic place where old pagan gods were worshipped. Considering all the facts, we can say that Prague Castle has served as a political and iconic center from time immemorial.

Christianity considerably changed political and social life in Bohemia; among other things, it considerably changed the principles of the Czech statehood. The Prague Castle area became the most sacred spot and the collective meeting place of the country, where pagan rituals were held. Then Prince Bořivoj usurped the area and had a Christian church built. He proclaimed himself a sovereign of God's will. A parallel can be seen here: there is just one God in the heavens and in the same way Bořivoj became the only ruler of his country and over all noblemen. It is no wonder that many problems arose. One of them - an uprising - Bořivoj only suppressed thanks to the support of

Romanesque Black Tower

Prince Svatopluk, the sovereign of the Great Moravian Empire. (Bořivoj was baptized at Svatopluk's court by the legendary archbishop St. Methodius).

The newly introduced statehood gradually did away with the old pagan symbols, e.g. the knight's seat, which had stood in the Prague Castle area since at least the 9th century AD and which was mentioned as late as 1142. This symbol of pre-Christian statehood then disappeared and the Czech Lands gained a new symbol – the eternal sovereign of the whole country, Prince **St. Wenceslas**. Wenceslas ruled during the 10th century

Přemysl Otakar I's gravestone by Petr Parléř

and he politically incorporated the Czech Lands into Western Europe. He also managed to get hold of remains of St. Vitus' and built a rotunda in the Prague Castle area for them; here he was later

Charles IV - bust from the triforium in St. Vitus' Cathedral

buried. He was assassinated by his brother Boleslav. In the year 929 or 935, Boleslav invited Wenceslas to a christening party. Wenceslas accepted and Boleslav killed him after the celebration in Stará Boleslav. Wenceslas was consecrated and became the main patron saint and protector of the Czech Lands; every Czech sovereign ruled and served solely on his behalf and all Czechs became Wenceslas' servants.

In 973 the Prague Bishopric was established and since that time on, the Slavic- Byzantine culture was pushed back by Latin and western tradition. This trend even strengthened after **St. Vojtěch** of the House of Slavníkovec was elected the second Prague Bishop in 983. He had a bishopric church built as a rotunda in the Great Moravian architectural style and this building became a shrine for the remains of the main Czech patron saints.

St. Vitus' Cathedral

The architectural style used became quite popular and we can trace its influence in the architecture of Czech churches to the 13th century. It even spread into neighboring countries and, in this way, the cultural and artistic style of the Great Moravian Empire was preserved; it survived the decay of the empire itself and the casting aside of the ancient Slavic alphabet, its culture, and eastern liturgy.

Bishop St. Vojtěch was one of the best-educated European scholars of that time. He studied in Magdeburg, where he made friends with a schoolmate, later Emperor Otto III. They both wanted to restore the Holy Roman Empire and strove hard to

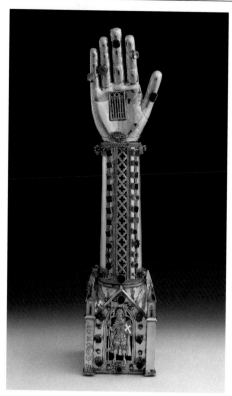

Shrine from the St. Vitus' treasure (14ᵗʰ century)

promote Christianity. Vojtěch's disciples brought Christianity to Poland and Hungary. The Czechs, however, did not sympathize much with Vojtěch's visions and his life was marked by constant conflicts between the Přemyslids and the House of Slavníkovec. When the enmity culminated in a massacre in which all members of the Slavníkovec family were slaughtered at their seat of Libice (995), St. Vojtěch emigrated, spent several years abroad, and died a martyr's death in Prussia (997).

In 1035, **Prince Břetislav** led Czech noblemen on a quest to Gniezdno (Poland), where Vojtěch's remains were

deposited. They brought the relics to Prague and buried them in the Bishop Church of St. Vitus, St. Wenceslas, and St. Vojtěch (biskupský kostel sv. Víta, Václava a Vojtěcha).

During their long history, the buildings of Prague Castle suffered numerous fires and reconstructions, but several holy places remained intact, e.g. St. Wenceslas' Grave (938).

The power of the Přemyslid dynasty culminated at the beginning of the 14ᵗʰ century when the dynasty united Central Europe, made Prague Castle its seat, and controlled Bohemia, Moravia, Silesia, Poland, Hungary (and shortly also the Alpine countries: 1250 – 1278). This great empire, however, fell apart after the last male member of the dynasty, **Wenceslas III**, was assassinated in Olomouc (1306).

Political chaos followed Wenceslas' III death and the situation only improved as late as under the rule of the **Luxembourg dynasty** (1310-1437). The King and Emperor **Charles IV** (†1378), whose mother Elizabeth was a Přemyslid princess, considered himself the true Přemyslid successor, followed Přemyslid ideas, and was nicknamed "Father of the Czech Nation." His activities shaped the Czech Lands, Prague, and Prague Castle quite considerably: he had the Royal Palace reconstructed and newly decorated (1333) and started the construction of St. Vitus' Cathedral (1344) on the occasion of raising the status of the Prague Bishopric to Archbishopric. He also reconstructed a stone bridge across the Vltava (after 1357), founded the New Town District

Rider's staircase – late Gothic (the so-called Vladislav's Gothic, about 1500)

Rudolph II's gravestone

(Nové Město) and the Prague University (1348), built fortifications in Lesser Town (Malá Strana) that have been partly preserved, etc. Under the rule of his son, **Wenceslas IV** (1378-1419), Czech art reached its peak, but at the same time serious and inextricable problems arose: a papal schism, civil war, the unrealistic ambitions of the king's relatives, and the beginning of the Czech Reformation (which began more than one hundred years before that of other European countries). Wenceslas' death triggered the Hussite Wars that isolated the Czech Lands from other European countries. The Hussites courageously and victoriously faced the dominance of the entire Catholic world and their heroism

Open space in front of St. George's Monastery – this place is linked to the oldest history of the Czech country

Entrance into the castle - Matthias's gate and Gate of Titans (in the front)

became a source of courage in times of suppression and inspired artists during the Czech National Revival in the 19th century. Hussite ideas became the model for future European Utraquists (Calixtines).

None of the future kings (not even the Hussite King **Jiří of Poděbrady** (1452 – 1471), a very competent man) managed to calm the situation completely and restore the former prosperity. Jiří of Poděbrady started negotiations with other European rulers in an attempt to establish an Assembly of European Sovereigns (1456-67) that would solve international conflicts in a peaceful way. However, he failed because other politicians and rulers did not trust a "heretic king".

The **Jagellonian dynasty** (1471-1526) managed to stop the civil wars (1485) and invasions from abroad (1490) step by step. Kings Vladislav II and Ludvík were both very ambitious but not very competent. They ruled over the Czech Lands and also over Hungary from 1490 and they tried to restore the glory of the Luxembourg era: they started vast building activities in Prague Castle and promoted late-Gothic and early-Renaissance art. However, their incompetence contributed to the decay of their power and resulted in their defeat at the battle of Mohacz (1526), where young King Ludvík perished. This disastrous defeat became a sad milestone in history: it opened the way for Turks, who invaded Hungary. For the Czech Lands, this meant the beginning of the **Habsburg** hegemony and this dynasty ruled over Central Europe for several centuries.

The **Habsburg dynasty** ruled over a vast empire (comprising Austria, the

Chapel of the Holy Cross and Baroque fountain by J. Kohl in the Second Courtyard

Czech Lands, and Hungary) for almost four hundred years (1526-1918). Their

Entrance to the Presidential Office (by B. Šípek)

time witnessed the flourishing Renaissance art and architecture, as can be seen at Queen Ann's Summer Residence. In 1541, a devastating fire damaged Prague Castle and the Lesser Town. The reconstruction work opened the way for Renaissance architecture and the development of horticulture. Reconstruction lasted for a long time and Prague once again reached its former glory under **Rudolf II** (1576-1611); under his rule Prague again became an international town and the center of European Mannerism. Rudolf made Prague Castle his residence and

16

accumulated the richest art collections of that time here. Rudolf, a "melancholy" sovereign, supported arts and sciences with great devotion. In 1609, he was forced to legalize freedom of faith. In his older age he suffered from madness, which brought an end not only to his rule but also to religious freedom. His Habsburg successors tended to support centralization and catholicization, which led to mounting political tension and consequently to the Uprising of the Czech Estates (1618-1620) and to the Thirty-Year War. During this war the Czech Protestants were defeated, Rudolf's collections were plundered, and the country was ravaged. Those people who refused to change faith lost their property and were forced to emigrate. The Czech Lands lost most of its native nobility, intelligentsia and patriciates. The war took a heavy toll on human life as just a half the original inhabitants remained in 1648. Prague Castle became the center of a province without any rights. Czech Baroque enriched the looks of the city but left almost no traces in the castle. **Maria Theresa** (1754-72), had the castle generously rebuilt. This fact did not, however, change the undignified position of the Czech Kingdom in the least. The exact opposite was true - Revivalist tendencies provoked and even strengthened the centralization policy of the Austrian government and the Germanization of the Czech Lands continued. As an answer to the situation, the few remaining Czech noble families started (together with the descendants of noble immigrants) to support the National Revival and the efforts to gain

Impluvium of the presidential flat (by J. Plečnik)

cultural and political independence. The National Revival culminated at the same time as work was being finished on St. Vitus' Cathedral (1859-1929) and finally led to political independence and to the proclamation of the Czechoslovak Republic (1918).

The modern period and modern art have left numerous traces in the Prague Castle complex, especially in the Cathedral. After the Czechoslovak Republic was proclaimed, the first president – **T. G. Masaryk** – entrusted Josip Plečnik, an individualistic architect, to make the residence the presidential seat. He did so in the most decent way and did not

Column Hall (by J. Plečnik)

THE WINGS OF THE NEW PALACE, THE FIRST AND SECOND COURTYARDS

For more that 1200 years, Prague Castle has served as a political base in the Czech state. In line with this, the New Palace today serves as the seat of the Presidential Office. The New Palace wings were built during 1763-71 by the Viennese court architect Nicola Pacassi. He managed to unite individual castle palaces (especially those from the time of Rudolf II) into one harmonious complex. The main entrance to the castle has always been located in the west, in Hradčany Square.

A ravine once used to separate the Prague Castle elevation from the adjacent Hradčany region. During the 10th

damage the historical charm of the place. The periods that followed – occupation by Nazi Germany (1939-45) and especially the era of the Communist dictatorship (1948-89) were not so merciful either to the architecture of Prague Castle, or to other historical sights. After democratic principles were restored in 1989, President **Václav Havel** started to renovate Prague Castle, the adjacent gardens, and the surrounding areas step-by-step.

Prague Castle is a place where a visitor can meet numerous architectural styles originating from different periods in close proximity to each other. These styles combine to form a typical, magnificent, original, and unmistakable complex that is a harmonious and living organism in which the present and the past meet.

Interior (by B. Šípek)

Spanish Hall

century, the ravine was transformed into a deep moat. In the 14th century two other moats were dug and the castle could be entered only by crossing the bridges until the 18th century. Nicola Pacassi filled the moats and thus created the First Courtyard in this way. This place serves as the courtyard of honor and is dominated by the **Gate of Titans,** which boasts the sculptural decorations of Ignac Platzer (1770-71). Another dominant feature is **Matthias' Gate** (1614), built in the late-Mannerist style. This gate was originally built into the Western Wing. Matthias' Gate is probably the work of Rudolf's architect Giovanni Maria Filippi, who built it at the order of Rudolf's brother and successor Matthias II. It shows many features of the Rudolf-era style and shows how the buildings at Rudolf's court may have looked.

The entranceway leading from Matthias' Gate divides the Western Wing into its southern and western parts. The interiors of the southern part were decorated in the Rococo style during the 18th century. The northern part is dominated by the monumental **Column Hall** (Sloupová síň), which was designed by **Josip**

Central Wing - Interior

Plečnik (1927-31). Plečnik's individual and yet sensitive style, which was always considerate to tradition, enchanted the first Czechoslovak president T. G. Masaryk and Plečnik became the presidential architect. The northern part of the Western Wing leads to the most monumental place of the presidential section of the castle – the **Spanish Hall** (Španělský sál). The impressive western entrance leads through a portico into the "Na Baště" garden (On the Bastion), also built by N. Pacassi. The Spanish Hall was built on the order of Rudolf II in 1602-1606 and court festivals and ceremonies were held here. The interiors were later re-decorated in the Baroque Revival style.

The Spanish Hall was built at the same time as the Northern Wing, where stables were located from the 16th century onwards. Today we can find the **Prague Castle Picture Gallery** here. Numerous works of art can be found in the places where thoroughbred Spanish horses were once boxed. These masterpieces are here to compensate for Rudolf's collections that were carried away shortly after Rudolf's death. The collections were partly deposited in Vienna, partly stolen by the Swedish army in 1648, and the last remains were sold by the enlightened Emperor Josef II. The present collections cannot compete with the Rudolf-era treasures, but nevertheless, they are a dignified successor (we can find here works by L. Cranach senior, H. Holbein junior, J. Seisenegger, P. Stevens, B. Spranger, H. von Aachen, Tizian, P. Veronese, Tintoretto, Bassano, D. Fetti, G. Reni, P. P. Rubens, and J. Kupecký).

The Northern Wing can be entered through the partly preserved **Northern Gate** (Severní brána). This gate leads to the Powder Bridge (Prašný most) that runs across Stag Moat (Jelení Příkop). This wing encloses the northern part of the Second Courtyard and from the east the courtyard is lined by the **Central Wing**. Rudolf II situated his famous "Art chamber" (Kunstkomora) here with many precious art collections. This place conceals Romanesque fortifications that date back to the 12th century. These fortifications were partly preserved and partly inbuilt into the complex together with the **White Tower** (Bílá věž) and the remains of the **Bishop Tower** (Biskupská věž). The White Tower used to serve as a prison, but Rudolf II had an armory built here – i.e. rooms for his collections

Obelisk of Mrákotín granite – Third Courtyard

Old Royal Palace – Gothic floor

of weapons. On the second floor of the White Tower, visitors can admire parts of the original Rudolf-era decorations in the shape of an allegoric fresco by the famous Bartholomew Spranger from the 1580s. We can only regret that this is the sole part to have been preserved.

Rudolf's private rooms were located in the Southern Wing of the Second Courtyard in the Summer Residence, which was rebuilt by Pacassi. The oldest Christian church in the Castle complex used to stand in the northwest part of the Second Courtyard, partly under the Western Wing – the famous Church of the Virgin Mary built by Prince Bořivoj (approx. 880). Today the courtyard is dominated by a **Baroque fountain by Jeroným Kohl** (1686), **a Renaissance well** with a decorative cover from the 18th century and **the Chapel of the Holy Cross** built by A. Lurago (1758-63) according to Pacassi's design. New interior decorations were made during the 19th century. Today the wings on the Second Courtyard are used for ceremonial purposes and the president's office is also here. J. Plečnik (1902-34) made several adjustments to the original Rococo and Classicist interiors by creating, for example, the **Impluvium** - the central room of the presidential apartments, the **Harp Room**, the **elevator** and others. The rooms were decorated by modern artists (e.g. Bořek Šípek, V. Havel's architect) and the place comprises both historical and modern art.

The passage in the Central Wing leads to the Third Courtyard, the historical center of Prague Castle.

Ludwig Wing

THE THIRD COURTYARD AND THE OLD ROYAL PALACE

The Third Courtyard and the Old Royal Palace are the most attractive places from the tourist's point of view. New reinforced concrete paving was laid here by Josip Plečnik. This enables archaeological work to continue under the surface without disturbing tourists and their sightseeing tours. The southern part of the courtyard is dominated by a **granite obelisk** (from the mines near Mrákotín). This monument was erected here in 1928 to commemorate the victims of the First World War. Another sight to attract visitors´ attention is the replica of a **bronze sculpture of St. George** (the original from 1373 is deposited in the National Gallery). Visitors can also admire the **Old Provost House** (Staré

Rooms of New Panels of the Czech Lands

Probošství), which was erected on the site of the Prague Bishop's Palace. The original complex (parts of the walls and a Romanesque window from 1142) was partly incorporated into the Provost House.

Hall of the Ludvík

the rule of Charles IV (after 1333). **The arcades** of the ground floor were open to the courtyard but were partly walled up under Wenceslas IV in around 1400. Many halls can be found behind the arcades: **a hall with a Romanesque fireplace** and remains of the warm-air heating system from the 15th century; **Charles' Hall,** which was created by joining together three smaller halls; the **Old Filing Department** – the accounting center of the Czech Kingdom; the **Column Hall of Wenceslas IV** (built in around 1400 in the Late gothic style), one of the most luxurious parts that was used for private royal purposes; and **the Hall of Court Files** (the ceiling was later rebuilt in the Renaissance style), where legal notices were kept. The **Chamber of Old Files of the Czech Lands**, a

The southern side of the Third Courtyard borders the **Old Royal Palace**. This complex is a multi-style architectural gem and its sections perfectly document the particular architectural styles and eras of Czech history. The underground rooms hide Romanesque halls over which a beautiful seat stood under the rule of Prince Soběslav (after 1135). The preserved cellar halls have cylindrical vaults and visitors can also see the remains of even older wall fortifications, probably from the 10th century. These rooms originally served as a storage place, wine cellars, and also as a prison in exceptional circumstances.

A **Gothic ground floor** was built over the Romanesque cellars during the Luxembourg era, and particularly under

Old Synod Hall

medieval safe where legal and property records were kept, is located in the northern wing. A **Late Gothic and Renaissance first floor** was erected over the Luxembourg Gothic ground floor during Jagellonian times (1471-1526). This was mainly used for state and political purposes.

The whole of the first floor is dominated by the late-Gothic **Vladislav's Hall**. This was built by Benedikt Ried (1486-1502), who joined three original Luxembourg halls into one space and

Vladislav's Hall - renaissance windows

created the biggest European vaulted interior without any inner supports. Of the original equipment, only three tin chandeliers have been preserved (16th century). Vladislav's Hall was used particularly for royal state purposes from the 16th century onwards. It was the scene of coronation festivities and banquets, knights' tournaments, and markets with artistic and luxurious goods. The architect B. Ried built Renaissance windows here, as well as in the adjacent **Rider's staircase**. Today the hall is used for state purposes – the presidential elections and the most important political and state ceremonies are held here. The Renaissance **Chamber of the Empire Court Council** is located above this hall. The original office furniture and a Dutch stove from the 17th century have been preserved here and in 1621, this was where the verdict was read to the leaders of the Protestant Uprising. From the southwest corner of Vladislav's Hall, a portal leads to the **Ludwik Wing**, which housed the offices of the **Czech Chancellery** – the central administrative body of the Czech Lands. On 23rd May 1618, the second room of the Chancellery witnessed the beginning of the Uprising of the Czech Estates: two governors (Jaroslav Bořita of Martinice, Vilém Slavata of Chlum and Košumberk) and their scribe (Filip Fabricius) were thrown from a window into the castle moat. This act (the protest against violating the freedom of the Czech Lands and freedom of faith) triggered the first conflict of the Thirty-Year War.

The northern wing is also accessible from Vladislav's Hall and consists of four

Vladislav's Hall - interior by B. Ried

rooms of **New Files of the Czech Lands** (from the 1560s). The original Renaissance furniture has been partly preserved and visitors can also admire rich murals depicting the coat-of-arms of the highest royal officials. The northern wing is dominated by the **Synod Hall**, where the meetings of the Synod of the

Church of All Saints

Czech Lands were held. A fire in 1541 completely destroyed its Gothic core and the Jagellonian vaults made by B. Ried. In the second half of the 16th century, Bonifác Wohlmut vaulted the room with new decorative ribbed vaults and renovated it in the historicist style. The present layout of the furniture corresponds to that of 1621, when the Restored Constitution of the Czech Lands was proclaimed here. Through this proclamation, the Czech Lands were deprived of rights and freedoms and this act crowned a huge number of previous cases of persecution. Consequently, the Protestant majority of the Bohemian population (90 %) was forced either to convert or to emigrate without any property.

A room called **the Entrance Hall** is located in the wing that stands over Wenceslas Column Hall. The Czech Chamber, a medieval Ministry of Finance, worked there. Next to it is **the Green Room**, where smaller trials were held and which is decorated with the coats-of-arms of the Chamber Court officials who held sessions here until the 18th century. The Czech Synod also used this place for its meetings. Two smaller halls are adjoined to the Green Hall: the late-Gothic style, so-called **Vladislav's Bedroom**, which is in fact a small audience chamber richly decorated with murals and masonry decorations (finished before 1490), and the Renaissance **Royal Court Hall** decorated with judges´ coats-of-arms from the 16th and 17th centuries.

The **Chapel of All Saints** is adjoined to the eastern part of the Palace. Its original Romanesque appearance dates

Vladislav's Bedroom

back to the 12th century and was replaced by the Gothic style in the 14th century (after 1370 by Petr Parléř, the architect of Charles IV). The major fire in 1541 destroyed the building to a substantial extent and only its peripheral walls remained. During restoration work (in 1580), the church was extended as far as the facade of Vladislav's Hall and was connected to the hall by means of a portal during later adaptations. The renovation costs were covered by the French Queen Elizabeth, widow of Charles IX (the sister of Rudolf II). The remains of St. Procopius were deposited here in 1588. St. Procopius founded the Sázava Monastery, where the masses were given in the old Slavic language till the end of the 11th century, and this saint was

St. Vitus' Cathedral – eastern view of the chorus

considered a patron of the Czech nation. Today the interiors are mostly Baroque in style (e.g. by V. V. Reiner) and the side-altar depicting holy angels was made by an artist from Rudolf's court (probably by Hans von Aachen).

St. VITUS´ CATHEDRAL

St. Vitus' Cathedral is the most sacred place of the Czech Lands, where the very heart of the Czech nation lies. The cathedral was erected in the Third Courtyard, in the place of the original

Triforium – bust of Petr Parléř

Romanesque St. Vitus' Rotunda (established by St. Wenceslas in 925). The Rotunda was later rebuilt in the shape of a Romanesque Basilica (after 1059). This holy place became the burial-site of the eternal sovereign and protector of the Czech Lands, St. Wenceslas. His tomb is situated in the **Chapel of St. Wenceslas,** which was finished in 1376 (built by Petr Parléř). It was incorporated in the cathedral as a separate architectural unit and is considered the most sacred place of the whole cathedral. Its square ground plan, quite unusual for its time, was designed so because it was unthinkable to move St. Wenceslas´ tomb. Unlike any other chapel in the Cathedral, this one is walled and enclosed. Its walls are covered with large, gleaming, precious stones and murals depicting the legend of St. Wenceslas (from the 16th century). There are also other precious sights: a 2-metre-high **statue of St. Wenceslas** (finished in 1373), murals depicting the Passions of Christ, and contemporary portraits of Charles IV and his fourth wife Elizabeth

of Pomerania. The chapel is vaulted with star-like vaults, a precious architectural element. The rest of the decorations are of Renaissance origin, except for a neo-Gothic gilded chandelier and the altar tombstone of St. Wenceslas from 1913.

The royal crown jewels are stored above the Chapel of St. Wenceslas. The most precious piece – the crown of St. Wenceslas – was made on the order of Charles IV. Legend has it that a person who puts this on his/her head without any right to do so will die within a year. The only person in history who did so

St. Vitus' Cathedral - interior

Chapel of St. Wenceslas

Statue of St. Wenceslas

himself (†1399) or by his sons and successors Jan and Wenceslas. The Great Tower was fitted with a Renaissance clock during the 16th century and Rudolf II donated a gilded grate to protect the largest Cathedral bell, which was known as Zikmund; it weighs 16 tons and was produced by Tomáš Jaroš in 1549.

A monumental entrance is situated between the Great Southern Tower and St. Wenceslas Chapel. This is called the **Golden Gate**. Its entrance space is vaulted in an unusual and complicated way by using, among other items, free ribs, i.e. construction supports in free, open space. This constructional element was used here in the 1360s, one hundred years earlier than in other European countries. The front face of the Golden Gate is decorated with **a mosaic** depicting Charles IV and his fourth wife, Elizabeth of Pomerania. The mosaic is the work of Venetian artists, who made it according to the design of Czech painters´ in 1371. It is considered to be the largest and oldest exterior mosaic in

was Hitler's protector R. Heydrich during the Second World War - he died after an assassination attempt by members of the Czech landing forces from Great Britain (1942).

The southern front of the Cathedral is dominated by the **Great Southern Tower,** which boasts a Renaissance walkway and a bulbous Baroque cupola. The core of the tower was built by Petr Parléř's workshop, as was the adjacent, open, **spindle-shaped staircase**, a masterly example of medieval engineering skills. The axis of the staircase changes its direction three times and the cladding of decorative ribs gives the whole construction an exquisite lightness. The staircase was designed by Petr Parléř

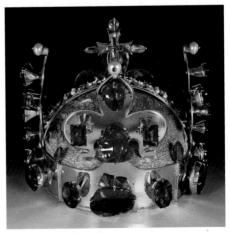

St. Wenceslas' royal crown

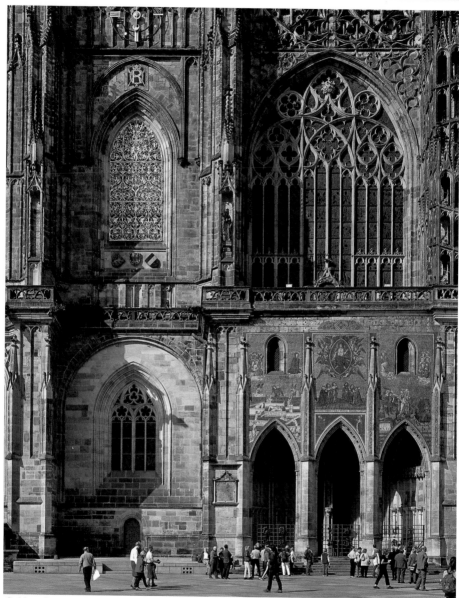

Golden Gate of the Cathedral

the region to the north of the Alps. Aggressive climatic conditions endangered this masterpiece but visitors can still admire it in its full original brilliance thanks to some recently completed restoration work.

P. Parléř and his workshop built part of the presbytery – up to the **Old Sacristy**.

Mosaic of the Last Judgement - detail

The Sacristy is vaulted in a daring way by using a suspension beam, a peak constructional element of the time (1356). Other remarkable architectural components can be found in the particular chapels for example the intricate window tracery in the Martinická Chapel (1360s) next to the Chapel of St. Wenceslas; such

Royal Oratory of Vladislav of the Jagellonian Dynasty (1493)

Old Sacristy - suspension bolting

Gravestone of Cardinal B. Schwarzenberg

a tracery was used here for the first time in Europe. The **presbytery vault** is another example of extraordinary engineering skills and is one of the oldest net vaults in Europe (finished in 1385). The craftsmen and engineers of the Cathedral workshop became inventors and pioneers not only in developing new architectural elements and technological procedures, but also in the architectural terminology of the 14th century (other Central European countries developed and enriched this terminology 50 or 100 years later). The sculptural decorations of Parléř's workshop are also of remarkable quality. We can say that the Cathedral became an imposing center of medieval sculptural art. We can find the **tombstones** of six Premyslid sovereigns and of Archbishop Jan Očko of Vlašim on the ground floor, **there are 21 portrait busts in the lower triforium, and the outer triforium** houses **10 busts of various saints**. The busts in the lower triforium are particularly unique – they not only depict members of the royal family and the highest clergymen, but also both architects of the Cathedral – Matthias of Arras and Petr Parléř – and five site engineers (it was not very common in the Middle Ages to portray architects and builders and this fact shows the somewhat liberal and pre-Renaissance character of Charles's IV court). The realistic appearance and perfect workmanship can surprise us even to this

Window panes by Alfons Mucha - detail

day. In 1619, during the Uprising of the Czech Estates, the Synod of the Czech Estates elected Friedrich of Paletinate to be Czech King (in Czech history he is also known as the „Winter King"). He arrived in Prague to be crowned here and some members of his suite, Protestant fanatics, partly damaged several statues by knocking their noses off. Friedrich did not understand much of the Czech Utraquist mentality, which was not so much radical as bigot Calvinist. Nevertheless, he ordered a stop to the iconoclasm in the Cathedral. The Uprising of the Estates is depicted in two pieces of a **wooden relief by J. Bechteler** (after 1630); one is deposited in the Valdštejn Chapel and the other on the opposite wall to the chancel, next to the Pernštejn Chapel. These depictions serve as a realistic source of information about the appearance of Prague and Prague Castle at that time.

Parts of the original wall paintings have been preserved in the presbytery chapels of the Cathedral - **Gothic murals** from the second half of the 14th century. These are as follows: Madonna on the Throne among Angels, Saints and Benefactors in the Chapel of the Holy Cross; Madonna with Benefactors in the Valdštejn Chapel; Painful Christ, Decapitation of St. Catherine, St. Vojtěch, Baptism of St. Otýlie, two portraits of Archbishop Jan Očko of Vlašim - all in the Vlašim Chapel - and Tribute of the Three Kings in the Saxon Chapel.

Remains of older buildings in the **Cathedral underground** remind us of its early history: e.g. the remains of the **Crypt of St. Cosma and St. Damian** in the eastern section. This crypt made up part of the original Romanesque Basilica from the 11th century. We can also admire the remains of the southern and northern apses that were discovered during archaeological excavations - the remains of the famous **St. Vitus' Rotunda** (founded by St. Wenceslas in 925). Visitors are mainly attracted by the **Royal Crypt,** where the burial tombs of Czech Kings and their consorts are stored. The crypt was built at the end of the 16th century and incorporated the remains of older Romanesque constructions. Its present-day architectural look is the work of K. Roškot (1928-35). The tomb of Charles IV (†1378) occupies the center of visitors' attention. We should also mention some of other Czech Kings who are buried here: Charles' son Wenceslas IV (†1419) and his wife Johana of

Bavaria; Ladislav the Posthumous (†1457); Jiří of Poděbrady (†1471); and Rudolf II (†1612), who is buried in the original, richly-decorated tin coffin.

After Petr Parléř, the ingenious architect, died in 1399, construction work slowed down and finally stopped during the Hussite Wars (1420). The centuries that followed added only minor parts to the unfinished cathedral. The Jagellonian dynasty built the late-Gothic **Royal Oratory** (1493) and the Habsburgs had the Renaissance **Royal Mausoleum** constructed. The Mausoleum preserves

Window panes by Karel Svolinský

Gravestone of St. John of Nepomuk

the tomb of Ferdinand I, Anna, and Maximilian II. After 1584, the polygonal **Chapel of St. Vojtěch** was erected in front of the temporary western part of the cathedral. This chapel was pulled down in the course of completion work (1873-1929). The Baroque era enriched the Cathedral with the **Tomb of St. John of Nepomuk** (1733-36), which is made of wrought silver.

The completion work on the Cathedral was directed by Josef Mocker (until 1899) and later by Kamil Hilbert. Both these architects managed to finish the complex in a sensitive way without damaging its original historical charm. The Cathedral interiors offered great opportunities to numerous Czech modern artists, for example, the famous **tomb of Cardinal B. Schwarzenberg** (1892-95) that was

Secession altar by František Bílek

made by Myslbek, the Secession and Symbolist **altar made by Fr. Bílek** (1899-1927), and **window panes** made by Fr. Kysela, M. Švabinský, A. Mucha, and other 20th century artists.

St. Vitus' Cathedral is not only the metropolitan Archbishop cathedral, but it is also the coronation site and burial-ground of Czech sovereigns. St. Wenceslas is its owner. The Cathedral has forever become the main symbol of Czech statehood, faith and the respect for St. Wenceslas that has been uniting Czech Protestants and Catholics for centuries.

ST. GEORGE´S CONVENT, VIKÁŘSKÁ and JIŘSKÁ STREET

In the year 920, Vratislav I, St. Wenceslas' father, established St. George's Basilica, one of the oldest buildings in the Prague

St. Vitus' Cathedral - portal in the western front

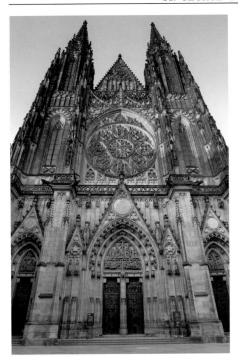

St. Vitus' Cathedral - western front

St. Vitus' Cathedral - interior

Castle area. Its present Romanesque appearance comes from the first half of the 12th century, when the church was reconstructed and enlarged. The early Baroque period left its mark in terms of the present-day striking façade. In 973, the **Benedictine St. George's Convent** was established here, thus incorporating the basilica into the complex. This oldest monastic house in the Czech Lands served as an education institution for Czech noble girls. Today its premises house the Baroque collections of the **National Gallery**. The most precious pieces are works by H. von Aachen, B. Spranger, A. de Vries (the artists at the court of Rudolf II), K. Škréta, P. J. Brandl, V. V. Reiner, F. M. Brokoff, and M. B. Braun, famous Czech Baroque painters and sculptors.

The medieval appearance and parts of the original interior decorations have been preserved in the **Chapel of St. Anna.** These are as follows: **the engraved tomb of the abbess Kunhuta of the Přemyslid dynasty** (†1321), the famous **St. George's altar** from the first half of the 15th century, the so-called **St. George's Tympanum** (a three-piece relief of Madonna with the Baby Jesus and Benefactors from the beginning of the 13th century), and the **insignia of the convent abbesses** (a staff and a crown).

43

St. George's Monastery (Old Royal Palace on the right)

The convent church guards the grave-tombs of several Přemyslid princes, e.g. Prince Vratislav (†921), who was the founder of the church, and his mother St. Ludmila (†921), who was St. Wenceslas' grandmother. Apse vaults in the main aisle and vaults in both side aisles are decorated with late-Romanesque murals from the beginning of the 13th century (Heavenly Jerusalem, Maiestas Domini). The Renaissance southern portal that leads into Jiřská Street is decorated with a tympanum depicting St. George killing a dragon (probably by B. Ried – 1515). The

Renaissance side entrance into St. George's Basilica - tympanum

Baroque Chapel of St. John of Nepomuk that is also joined to the church (by F. M. Kaňka – 1718-22) is decorated with murals by V.V. Reiner.

St. George's Square is situated in front of the western part of the church. This was the mythical place where the ancient seat of Czech knights used to stand between the 9th and the 12th centuries. It was made of stone and Czech princes were "enthroned" on it. The seat was mentioned as late as 1142 and then all traces disappeared. The northern side of the square, the neo-Gothic buildings of the **New Provost's Residence** (by Josef Mocker – 1879-81), continues into Vikářská Street which runs around the northern part of the Cathedral. The

St. George's Basilica – Romanesque interior

Apse of the St. George's Basilica; on the right - gravestone of Prince Vratislav I, the founder of the basilica

cloister wings of St. Vitus' Monastery and a chapter house used to stand here until the second half of the 14th century. The cloister complex was pulled down during Gothic reconstruction activities. Vikářská (Vicar) Street was named after the Romanesque house of **"Stará Vikárka" (Old Vicarage)** which was rebuilt several times. This house originally served as the residence of the cathedral's vicars, but it was rebuilt into a pub in the first half of the 19th century, in which form it has prospered here to this day. Czechs are familiar with this place thanks to the writer Svatopluk Čech, who based the plots of his books here.

Supreme Burgraviate

The Renaissance building next door was originally used as a **steel foundry** (built after 1541) where cannons were cast until the 18th century. Stables were situated here between 1723 and 1918 and later the building also became a pub.

The other buildings in Vikářská Street are mainly Renaissance in character, although some of them were later adapted and re-built (e.g. **Mladota's House** – originally a Chapter Deanery, where the Jagellonian architect B. Ried lived).

Vikářská Street runs towards the **northern fortifications,** where visitors

Prague Castle – view from Queen Anna's Summer Palace

Golden Lane

are attracted by the **Mihulka artillery tower** (built by B. Ried at the end of the 15th century). Mihulka never served military purposes and was used as a residential building. Among others T. Jaroš, the bronze-smith who cast the cathedral's biggest bell, lived here. During the Rudolf era, . alchemist workrooms were located here and the place was later changed into a gunpowder store, which exploded in 1645. Nevertheless, the massive construction survived the explosion without severe damage.

Jiřská Street runs along the southern corner of St. George's Convent. A Classicist building - the **Institute of Noblewomen** - can be seen opposite the convent. It was built after 1753 (according to the design of N. Pacassi) in the place of the original Renaissance Rosenberg Palace (it was built under the direction of Ulriko Aostalis, a Rudolf-era architect, in 1573). The Institute was abolished after the Czechoslovak Republic was proclaimed and since that time it has served as an administrative building. Jiřská Street also runs along Lobkowicz

Powder Tower - Mihulka

Palace and the Renaissance-style Supreme Burgraviate (1555) and leads us to the Romanesque Black Tower. **Lobkowicz Palace,** originally the seat of the Pernštejn family, underwent several reconstructions and today we can admire its final appearance – a Renaissance palace adapted in the Baroque style. The palace today houses several of the collections of the National Museum and an exhibition of Czech history.

The **Supreme Burgraviate** (a medieval "presidium of the government") was profoundly reconstructed, but the interiors partly retained their original Renaissance character. The Romanesque **Black Tower** from 1135 served as a prison, which was very common for the

towers of Prague Castle. Next to the Black Tower is the Renaissance **Eastern Gate**, which was built after 1560. This gate leads to the **Old Castle Stairs** (Staré zámecké schody), to the Lesser Town (Malá Strana) and to **Opyš.** In

Southern Gardens

49

Garden of the Riding Stables of Prague Castle

Opyš, a beautiful gazebo is now found in the place of the original fortifications. From here visitors can enjoy a magnificent view of Prague. It was from here also that a cannon was fired to mark midday. **St. Wenceslas' Vineyard** stretches out between the Old Castle Stairs and Na Opyši Street. Legend has it that St. Wenceslas himself founded this vineyard way back in the 920s.

We can use Jiřská Street to get to **Golden Lane,** which is a famous and picturesque Prague street. Its tiny Renaissance houses, most often single-storied, were inserted into the semicircular arches of Romanesque fortifications. This shows us how the castle servants and castle garrison lived. Archers resided here from 1591 onwards and the lane later became a center of goldsmithery. It is also famous for being Franz Kafka's temporary living place (1916-17).

Any visitor's attention is mainly attracted by the fortification towers, one

Bellevue Pavilion

"Na Valech" Garden (former Rosenberg Palace)

of which is worthy of note. The **White Tower** was built in the late 15th century. Rudolf II transformed it into a prison in 1585 and relocated the torture chamber and dungeon that were originally placed in the Central Castle Wing in the Romanesque tower of the same name (the Castle White Tower was changed into an armory where Rudolf kept his collections of weapons). The best-known tower - **Daliborka** (1496) is famous for being the prison in which Dalibor of Kozojedy was imprisoned during Jagellonian times (1498). Bedřich Smetana, a Czech famous composer, depicted this story in an opera called Dalibor. Both Daliborka and White

Tower were used as prisons until the second half of the 18th century.

THE GARDENS OF PRAGUE CASTLE

Prague Castle is surrounded by numerous **gardens** [the Na Baště Garden (on the Bastion), the Rajská zahrada (Garden of Eden), the Na Valech Garden (on the Ramparts), Jelení příkop (Stag Moat), and Královská zahrada (the Royal Garden)]. These gardens have been cultivated since the time of Ferdinand I (1534) and are decorated with many Renaissance and Baroque sculptures created by famous artists (e.g. M. B. Braun). From the very beginning, buildings for the entertainment of court society were built here, for example, the Baroque **Riding School** of J. B. Mathey (built at the end of the 17th century). This Riding School has been used as an exhibition building since 1948. The Renaissance **Ball Games Hall** was constructed by B. Wohlmut and was the oldest walled sport building in Europe (finished in 1569).

Other interesting complexes can be found in close proximity to the castle, e.g. **Lion Court**. This replaced the old menagerie in 1581 and beasts of prey

Queen Anna's Summer Palace with the Singing Fountain

Renaissance Ball Games Hall (1569)

were kept here until the second half of the 18th century. Together with the exotic animals, exotic flora was also cultivated here and we can enjoy the exotic plants and rare wood species to this day. The Royal Gardens witnessed the first blossom of tulips that Rudolf II had imported from Holland in 1557. Rudolf II had also a walled orangery incorporated in the complex. The British-Czech architect Eva Jiřičná created the **New Orangery** from the fragments of the original building between 1995 and 1998. This is a technical wonder of modern times.

Queen Anna's Summer Palace is the most famous building in the Royal Garden. Ferdinand I (1535-63) had this building constructed for his wife, Anna of

Hercules's Fountain

Bull Staircase

Orangery by E. Jiřičná

the Jagellonian dynasty. Its architects P. della Stella, G. Spatio, and B. Wohlmut managed to create a stylistically pure construction which was considered a true revolution in Central Europe, and was justly described as a jewel in the crown of the trans-alpine Renaissance. It is decorated with dozens of Renaissance murals depicting historical motifs. The bronze **Singing Fountain** in front of the Summer Palace was built in 1564 by the bell-maker and gunsmith Tomáš Jaroš according to the design of the court painter Francesco Terzio. The melodic sound of falling water apparently gave the fountain its name.

The Renaissance-style Royal Garden is a true gem, but we should not forget to mention the other remarkable gardens:

the **Southern Garden** (Jižní zahrada) and the **Garden on the Ramparts** (Na Valech). These were both founded in 1559 and have undergone many adaptations. They have been open to the public since 1991. Their modern-day appearances were designed by J. Plečnik after 1920. The main entrance to the gardens is situated on Hradčany Square and they are connected to the Third Courtyard via **Bull Staircase** (Býčí schodiště). The gardens are richly decorated and here we can find a large, one-piece, granite **round bowl** made of Mrákotín granite, an **arenaceous marl pyramidal spire,** and several pavilions, e.g. **Bellevue.** Two limestone obelisks mark the spot where two governors were thrown out of the window during the events in Prague in

"On the Ramparts" Garden

Royal Garden – view from the St. Vitus' Cathedral

1618. Surprisingly, they were not harmed at all. One source (the Protestant chronicler Pavel Skála of Zhoř) says that they fell on a dumping ground, whilst the other, Catholic sources say that they were rescued thanks to the Virgin Mary's help. The garden contains many other interesting architectural and sculptural elements, both of Baroque and modern origin.

The first Czechoslovak president's idea was to give the castle and its surroundings a democratic character, which became the task of J. Plečnik, whose architectural style can be traced and admired here. Plečnik connected the garden complexes and created a bypass around Prague Castle. He connected the Garden on the Bastion with the Powder Bridge, and the Southern Garden with Hradčany Square, the Castle Courtyards, and the eastern foreland. This large area, which Czech people see as a sacred piece of land, is full of plants, trees, and elegant architectural and sculptural elements. The gardens have preserved their luxurious character but are now open to the public. President Václav Havel also showed great endeavor in an attempt to continue the Masaryk tradition.

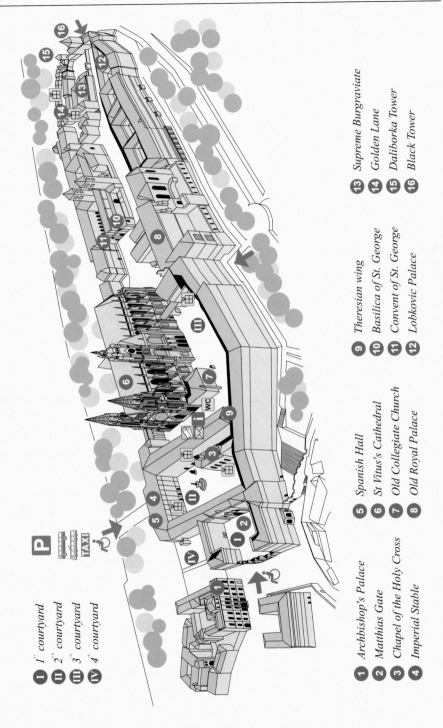

1 *1'' courtyard*
2 *2'' courtyard*
3 *3'' courtyard*
4 *4'' courtyard*

1 *Archbishop's Palace*
2 *Matthias Gate*
3 *Chapel of the Holy Cross*
4 *Imperial Stable*
5 *Spanish Hall*
6 *St Vitus's Cathedral*
7 *Old Collegiate Church*
8 *Old Royal Palace*
9 *Theresian wing*
10 *Basilica of St. George*
11 *Convent of St. George*
12 *Lobkovic Palace*
13 *Supreme Burgraviate*
14 *Golden Lane*
15 *Daliborka Tower*
16 *Black Tower*

THE CZECH CROWN JEWELS

The Czech crown jewels are stored in the Coronation Chamber of St. Vitus' Cathedral under the protection of St. Wenceslas. The chamber can be entered from St. Wenceslas' Chapel, but its door is provided with seven locks and can only be opened if the seven key-holders are present.

The crown was made on the order of Charles IV and was dedicated to St. Wenceslas. It was used for the first time in 1347 when Charles was crowned Czech King. The crown was purposely made in a rather archaic shape to follow in the footsteps of the older Přemyslid tradition and to evoke the history of Czech statehood and respect for predecessors. The crown is 19 cm wide, 19 cm high and weighs 2 358.3 grams. It is made of the purest gold (21-22 carats) and is decorated with 96 unique-quality, precious stones (sapphires, spinels, rubies, emeralds) and 20 pearls. The cross at the top of the crown is decorated with a sapphire cameo where a relief of the Crucifixion from the 13th century is placed.

The scepter and the orb, exquisite examples of Renaissance goldsmith mastery, probably date back to the first half of the 16th century. They were made of very pure gold and are decorated with sapphires, spinels, and pearls. The orb is 220 millimeters in height and weighs 780 grams. It is decorated with a hammered relief depicting scenes from the bible. The scepter is 670 millimeters in length, it weighs 1013 grams, and it is decorated with intricate plant motifs. The headpiece was made in the shape of a blossom.

Czech royal crown jewels, symbol of the Czech, more than ten centuries long, statehood

SOVEREIGNS OVER THE CZECH LANDS AND PRAGUE CASTLE

Era of the Princes of Přemyslid Dynasty
Bořivoj (880-894) – the first Christian Prince in Bohemia; resided in Prague Castle; founded the Church of the Virgin Mary
Spytihněv (894-915) – released the Czech Lands from the hegemony of the Great Moravian Empire
Vratislav I (915-921) – founded St. George's Church in the Prague Castle area (after around 910)
St. Wenceslas (921-935) – founded St. Vitus' Rotunda in the Prague Castle area (approx. 926); was consecrated
Boleslav I (935-967) – built the early Czech state and enlarged its territory; supported Otto I in the wars against the Hungarian army at the battle of Lech (955)
Boleslav II (967-999) – founded the Prague Bishopric and St. George's Benedictine Convent; united the empire and enlarged its territory; massacred the Slavníkovec House (995)
Boleslav III (999-1002, 1003)
Vladivoj (1002-1003) – came from the Piastovec dynasty (relatives of the Přemyslid dynasty)
Boleslav the Valiant (1003-1004) – a Polish Prince from the Piastovec dynasty (the grandson of Boleslav I)
Jaromír (1003/4-1012, 1034), Oldřich (1012-1034)
Břetislav (1034-1055) – brought St. Vojtěch's remains from Poland; introduced the succession order of Czech rulers
Spytihněv II (1055-1061) – constructed St. Vitus' Cathedral (the Basilica of Spytihněv)
Vratislav II (1061-1092) – was awarded the title of the Czech King in 1085 (for himself)
Konrád I of Brno (1092), Břetislav II (1092-1100), Oldřich of Brno (1100)
Bořivoj II (1101-1107, 1117-1120), Svatopluk (1107-1109), Vladislav I (1109-1125)
Soběslav I (1125-1140) – began to reconstruct Prague Castle
Vladislav II (1140-1173) - was awarded the title of the Czech King in 1158 (as a reward for his help in the crusade against Milan)
Soběslav II (1173-1178) – finished the reconstruction of Prague Castle
Oldřich (1173), Bedřich (1172-1173, 1178-1189)
Konrád III Ota (1189-1191) – issued the oldest Legal Code written in the Czech language (known as the Statute of Konrád Ota)
Václav II (1191), Jindřich Břetislav (1193-1197), Vladislav Jindřich (1197)

Era of Kings of the Přemyslid Dynasty and the Time of Prosperity
Přemysl Otakar I (1192-1193, 1197-1230) – gained the hereditary title of Czech King (1198); 1212 rights of the Czech Kingdom were ratified
Václav I (1230-1253) – political, economic, and cultural prosperity
Přemysl Otakar II (1253-1278) – the "King of Gold and Iron"; economic prosperity; founded numerous towns in Bohemia and Austria; founded the Land Court
Václav II (1283-1305) – king of the Czech Lands and Poland; Czech kings gained the elector's title; started to coin Prague Groschens (1300)
Václav III (1305-1306) – king of the Czech Lands, Poland and Hungary (Ladislav V); the Přemyslid dynasty died out after his assassination

Era of the Luxembourg Dynasty and the Beginning of the Czech Reformation
Jindřich of Carinthia (1306, 1307-1311), Rudolf of Habsburg (1306)
Jan of Luxembourg (1310-1346) – king of the Czech Lands and Poland; prioritized foreign policy; was killed at the battle of Crécy
Karel IV (1346-1378) – king of the Czech and German Lands; Emperor of the Holy Roman Empire

since 1355; a leading European sovereign of the late Middle Ages; founded many institutions; supported the development of Prague and Prague Castle; issued the Golden Bulla code (the code of law of the Holy Roman Empire); issued the coronation order

Václav IV (1378-1419) – king of the Czech Lands and Rome; conflicts with high nobility (Noblemen Union) and the church; supported the reformation tendencies of the church

Zikmund of Luxembourg (1419-1437) – king of Hungary (from 1387), king of Rome (from 1410), king of the Czech Lands (from 1419), Roman Emperor (from 1433); tried to reform the church; organized crusades

Albrecht II of Habsburg (1437-1439), Ladislav the Posthumous (1453-1457)

Jiří of Poděbrady (1458-1471) – efforts to create a union of European sovereigns to solve conflicts in a peaceful way; first wars with the Hungarian king Matthias Korvin

Era of the Jagellonian Dynasty

Vladislav II (1471-1516) – king of the Czech Lands, king of Hungary (from 1490; he resided in Budin = Budapest from that time on); period of the so-called "Vladislav Gothic era"

Ludvík (1516-1526) – king of the Czech Lands and Hungary; died at the battle of Mohacs

Era of the Habsburg Dynasty

Ferdinand I of Habsburg (1526-1562) – king of the Czech Lands and Hungary, king of Rome (from 1531), German-Roman Emperor (from 1556); centralization and re-catholicization tendencies

Maximilian II (1562-1575) – king of the Czech and German Lands, king of Hungary (since 1563), Roman Emperor (since 1564); beginning of religious liberty

Rudolf II (1575-1611) – Prague became the Emperor's seat and the center of late-Mannerism

Mathias (1611-1617) – Vienna became the sovereign's permanent seat

Ferdinand II (1617-1619, 1620-1627) – suppressed the Uprising of the Czech Estates, gained absolute power, the Czech Lands became the hereditary possession of the Habsburg Dynasty

Friedrich of Paletinate (1619-1620) – was elected Czech King by the rebellious Czech Estates (called "the Winter King")

Ferdinand III (1627-1646, 1654-1656) – forcible re-catholicization

Ferdinand IV (1646-1654), Leopold I (1656-1705), Josef I (1705-1711)

Charles VI (1711-1740) – pragmatic sanctions (gained succession for the Habsburg-Lorraine Dynasty)

Maria Theresa (1740-1780) – introduced reforms (e.g. compulsory education); grand-scale reconstruction of Prague Castle

Josef II (1780-1790) – liberal absolutist; introduced reforms (e.g. the Patent of Tolerance – guaranteed freedom of faith, abolition of serfdom)

Leopold II (1791-1792)

František I (1792-1835) – the Holy Roman Empire split up; the Austro-Hungarian Empire still existed

Ferdinand V (the Benevolent) (1835-1848) – the last sovereign to be crowned Czech King

František Josef I (1848-1916) – the sovereign who ruled for the longest time

Karel I (1916-1918)

Presidents since the proclamation of the Czechoslovak Republic (1918)

Czechoslovak Republic: Tomáš Garrigue Masaryk (1918-1935), Edvard Beneš (1935-1938, 1945-1948); Protectorate of Bohemia and Moravia (occupation by Nazi Germany): Emil Hácha (1938-1945); Czechoslovak Socialist Republic (communist dictatorship): Klement Gottwald (1948-1953), Antonín Zápotocký (1953-1957), Antonín Novotný (1957-1968), Ludvík Svoboda (1968-1975), Gustáv Husák (1975-1989); Czechoslovak Federal Republic and Czech Republic after November 1989: Václav Havel (1989-2003), Václav Klaus (since 2003)

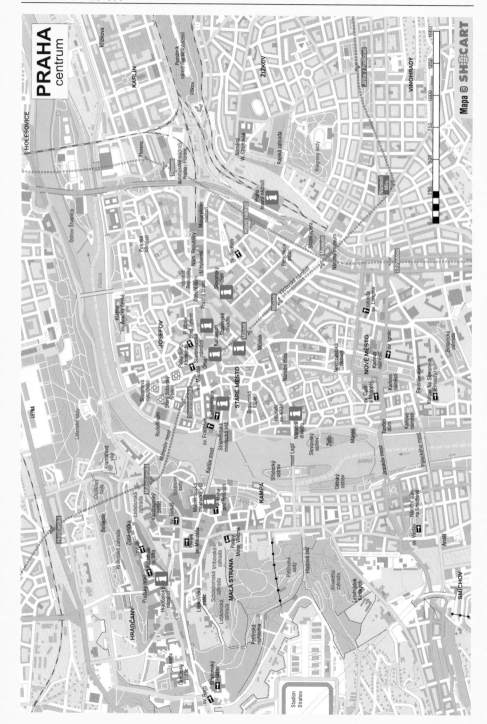

TOURIST INFORMATION CENTRES

ℹ Celetná 14, Prague 1
phone, fax: + 420/224 491 764
e-mail: info@aroundprague.com
OPEN DAILY: 9.00 a. m. - 8.00 p. m.

ℹ Laterna Magika
Národní 4, Prague 1
phone, fax: +420/224 901 166,160
e-mail: info.laterna@quick.cz
OPEN DAILY: 9.00 a. m. - 8.00 p. m.

ℹ Karlova 1, Prague 1
phone, fax: +420/221 663 105,106
phone: +420/724 249 624
e-mail: info.karlova@quick.cz
OPEN DAILY: 9.30 a. m. - 8.30 p. m.

Our information Centres offer you:

- Tickets, Prague Cards ■ Last Minute Accommodation ■ Sightseeing Tours & Trips

- Guided Walks

- Free Guidebooks "Around Prague"
  in English, French, German, Italian, Spanish, Russian and Japanies

- Guidebooks, Maps, Travel Pass ■ Rent a car

www.aroundprague.cz

HOTEL ČERTOVKA

★★★★
PRAHA

*Hotel Čertovka is originally a baroque house, it has recently
been refurbished. It is situated in Lesser Town, close
to the Charles Bridge. The rooms have a view
of the bridge and panorama of Hradčany,
the Prague Castle, and the Bridge Tower.*

*The Hotel offers accommodation in 16 double rooms and 5 single rooms
with every comfort and breakfast buffet, both cold and hot.
Every room is equipped with satellite programme television,
a minibar, hair dryer, telephone and a safe.
In the neighbourhood of Hotel Čertovka,
here are many various restaurants, cafés and wine bars,
and our helpful staff will gladly make
a recommendation.*

U Lužického semináře 2, Praha 1 - 118 00, Czech Republic
Tel:+ 420 257 532 235, + 420 257 011 500, Fax:+ 420 257 534 392
E-mail: reservations@certovka.cz, www.certovka.cz